MIRACLE ON THE HUDSON

MIRACLE ON THE HUDSON

COLORING BOOK

WRITTEN &
ILLUSTRATED
by CAROLYN MACY

  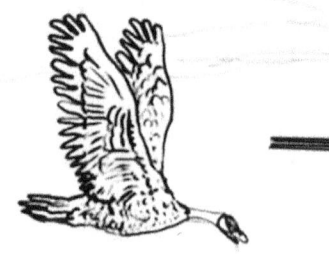

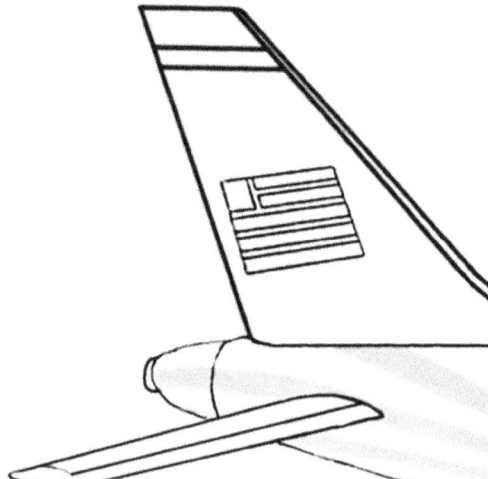

Miracle on the Hudson - Coloring Book
Copyright © 2017 by Carolyn Macy. All rights reserved.

No part of this publication may be reproduced, stored in a retrieval system or transmitted in any way by any means, electronic, mechanical, photocopy, recording or otherwise without the prior permission of the author except as provided by USA copyright law.

Published by Carolyn Macy
6227 81st Avenue N.E. | Norman, Oklahoma 73026 USA
405.401.2012

Book design copyright © 2017 by Carolyn Macy.
Written and Illustrated by Carolyn Macy

Published in the United States of America
ISBN: 978-0-9989127-6-9
1. JUVENILE NONFICTION / Biography & Autobiography / Historical
2. JUVENILE NONFICTION / Transportation / Aviation

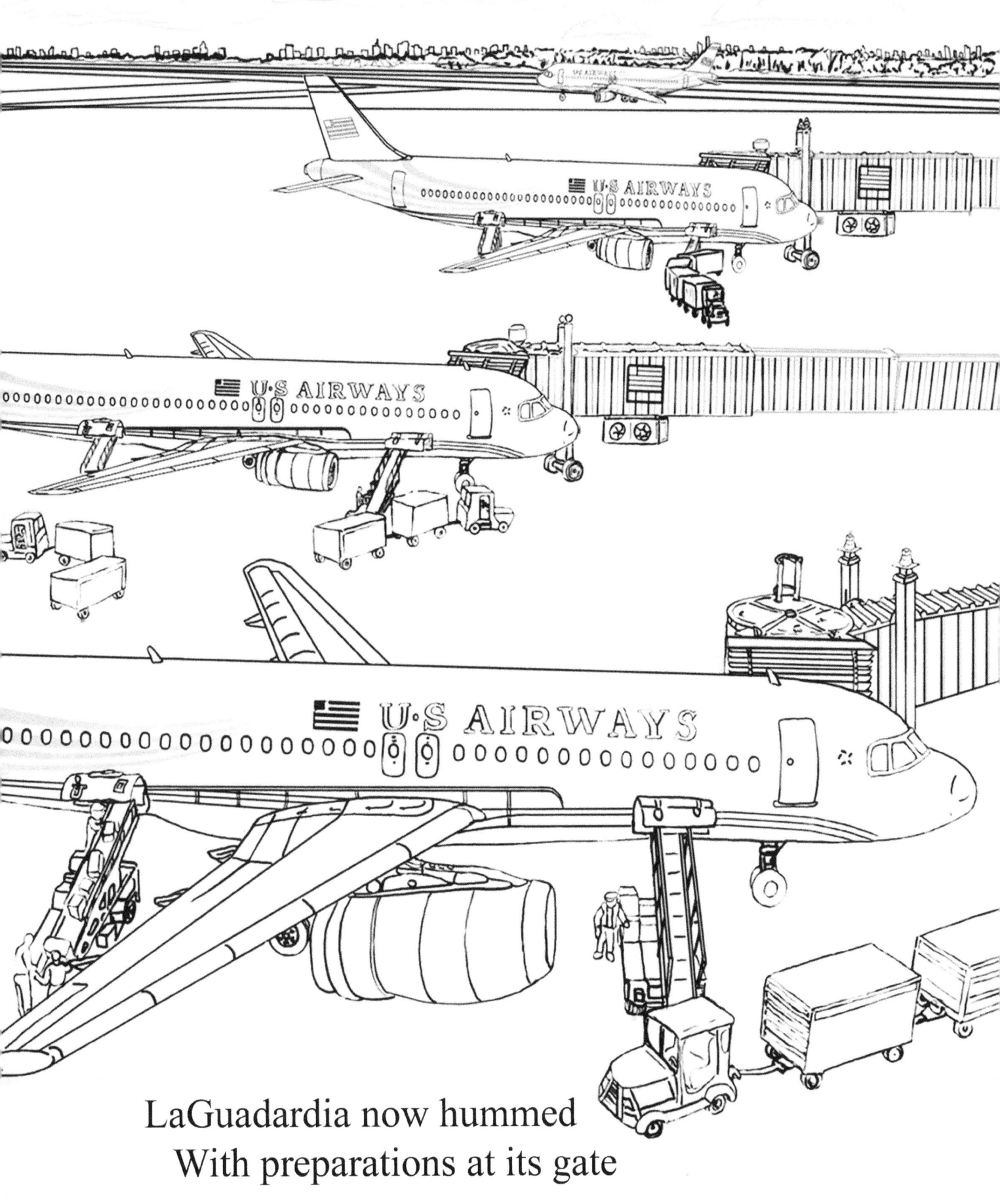

LaGuadardia now hummed
With preparations at its gate

As things sometimes do come to pass,
A flock of geese did fly

Into the path flown by the plane
And struck it in the sky.

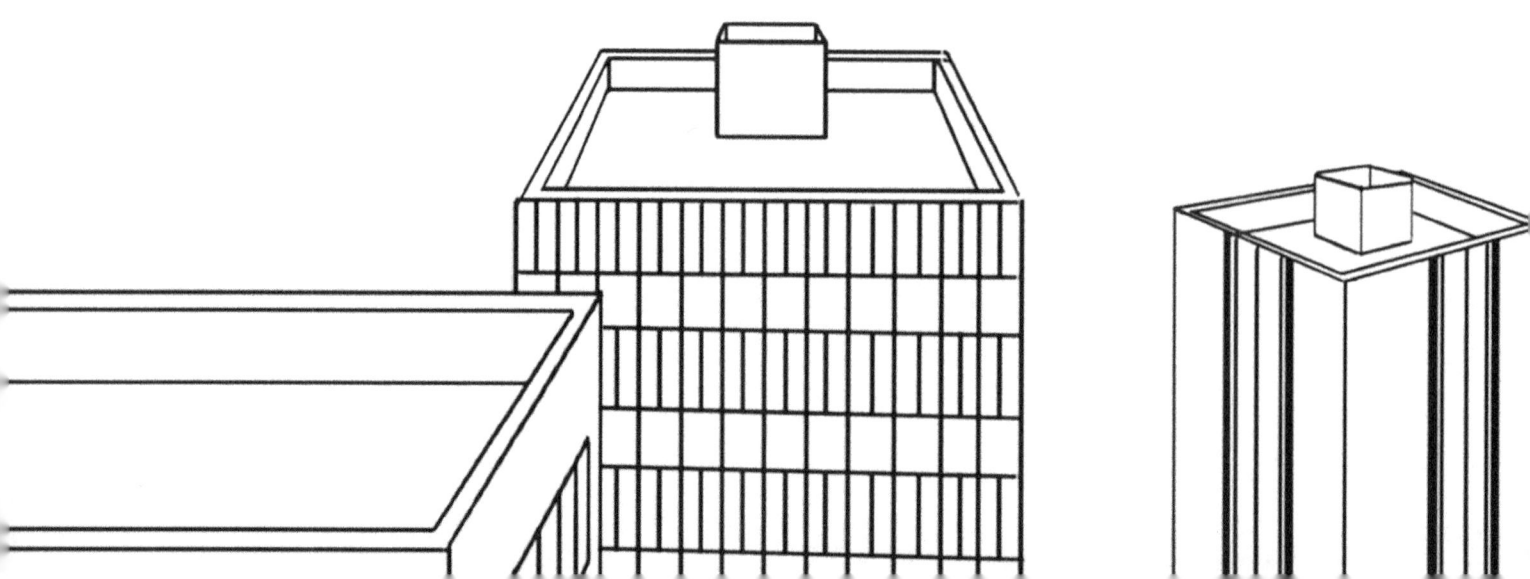

Now flying upward in the sky
To leave the airport just behind,
There Captain Sully flew his craft
With course for flight assigned.

As things sometimes do come to pass,
A flock of geese did fly

Into the path flown by the plane
And struck it in the sky.

Their strike made both the engines quit
Which caused the plane to slow,
And glide on from that moment
Over skyline just below.

With Little time for protocol
And little time to think,
His skill and wisdom learned through time
Helped hold the plane in sync.

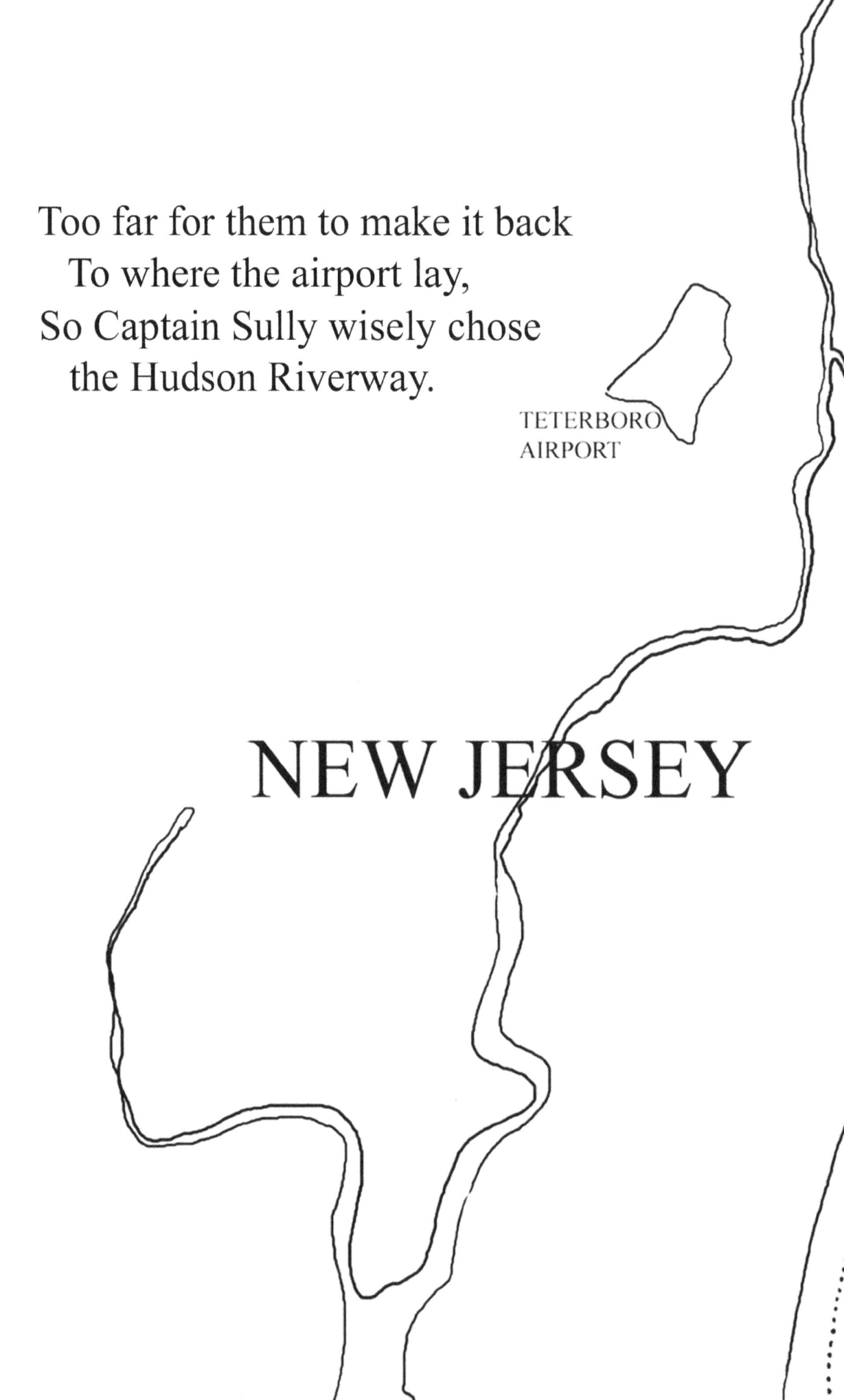

Too far for them to make it back
   To where the airport lay,
So Captain Sully wisely chose
   the Hudson Riverway.

TETERBORO
AIRPORT

NEW JERSEY

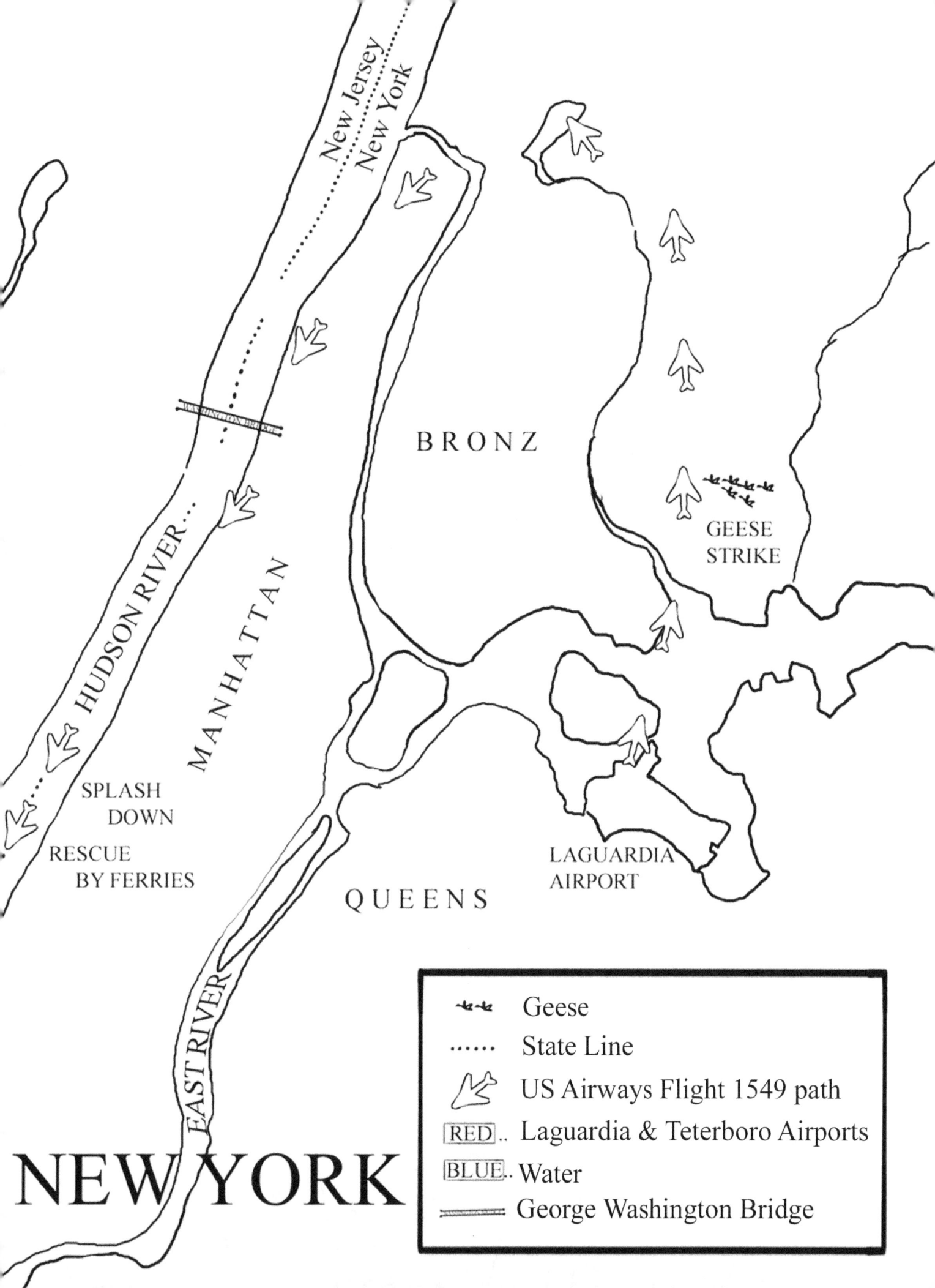

Still fastened in their seats
 With watchful worry while they wait,
 Those folks grabbed life vests to be worn
 With little hurry to inflate.

Now heading for their river stop
With hopes of landing whole,

All those aboard sat calmly braced
And praying for their soul.

Just gliding with the wings held straight,
The nose raised up, but not too much,
And flaps turned down to slow the craft,
He made the tail the first to touch.

He landed on the Hudson
After splashing to a stop
And landed safely in one piece
From their untimely drop.

The pilot, Captain Sully,
   In his craft with crew of five
And all one hundred fifty souls
   Survived to land alive!

The river showed good will
To all those there that day
Who slowly floated down
Its chilly waterway.

Those folks aboard this flight
Then faced another threat.
The plane began to sink,
And folks grew cold and wet.

Their rescue by near ferryboats,
Those folks now numb with cold,
Were seen by some on shore
Who watched it all unfold.